when heart cries...

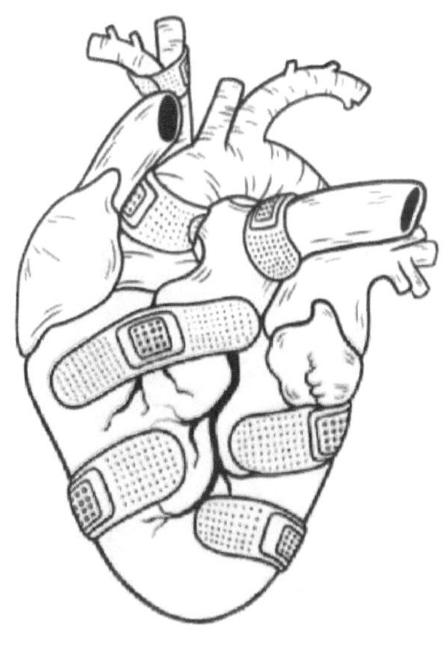

RAVI RAHUL

to the lady who built my heart with her blood
to make me feel this world..

and

to those feelings of this heart who made me
write these words..

Acknowledgement

In the journey of birthing this book, I've been fortunate to have some amazing souls by my side, and now it's time to give credit where it's due.

Big shout-out to Gunjan – the proofreading superhero. Your keen eye and dedication turned my words into something polished and beautiful. Thanks for making sure every comma was in its happy place.

To the incredible artists whose work graces these pages – your creations added a whole new dimension to my words. Your talent is the brushstroke that brought this book to life.

To my friends, the real MVPs of this journey. Your encouragement was the wind beneath my wings. Thanks for pushing me when I needed it and being that steady anchor when self-doubt came knocking.

And to the one who helped me unearth these feelings – you know who you are. Thanks for being the emotional archaeologists, digging deep with me and helping me discover the stories hidden in my heart.

This book is as much yours as it is mine.

-Ravi Rahul

Preface

Are there enough words to describe human emotions?

There're more than 8 billion hearts, and there're roughly 1 million words in the most common language in the world.

Not all emotions are the same. Same types of emotions can vary person to person.

So, here I am, giving it a shot. My first try putting it all in these pages – my attempt to pin down those feelings and turn them into words. It's not some big show; it's like sharing a slice of my heart. I won't pretend I've got all the fancy words, but who knows, we might stumble onto something that clicks.

Consider this your invite to dive into the language of the heart together. Feel the words, feel the emotions. This is my humble attempt to share a bit of what's inside, and I hope it connects with something inside you too.

Cheers to emotions, words, and the magic that happens when they dance together.

-Ravi Rahul

Miracle Happens

I have seen in movies -
miracle happens,
after all the odds,
love wins..

but seems these miracle happens,
only in movies..

इश्क

इश्क लेकर अपना
इश्क ढूंढने आया था मैं
इश्क में

सब मिला मुझे
सिवाए
इश्क के

When heart cries

Eyes stop responding to heart,
after a period of time.

they don't shed tears,
when heart cries..

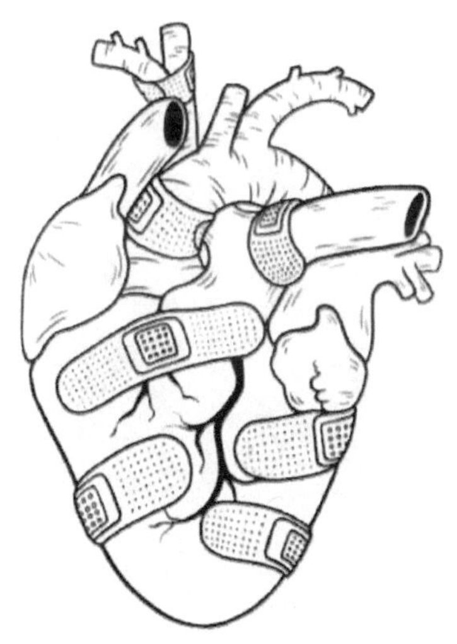

Rear-view Mirror

In the journey of life,
memories & experiences
work as rearview mirror..

By looking into it,
We define our next moves..

11:11

The day I won't remember you,
When I see 11:11,
That day I will think I've moved on..

दुआएं

किसने कहा दुनिया में सस्ता कुछ भी नहीं ?
दुआएं आज भी मिलती हैं सिक्को के भाव
सड़क किनारे..

Parallel Universe

It is said that there are 7 parallel universes..
I want to travel to all of them,
with hope to find myself in your arms,
not in this, but at least in one of them,
I might be lucky..

Courage

It takes courage to live,
but it takes more courage to end the life..

May be because we just have to think
of our suffering while we choose to live.

But we have to consider about the sufferings
of our loved ones when we choose to end it.

The sufferings they will get after our demise
is way too much than we can even imagine,

And our pains create an illusion..
The illusion in which we don't see who are connected to us.

What is Success?

For some it's million dollar mansion,
For some just fulfilled passion..

Some call it getting their dream cars,
While some, getting rid of their deep scars..

You may get success if u get your dream partner in life,
I may get success if I survive the next 5 years in life..

For some it may be a diamond piece,
While some are just looking for heart in peace..

For some it can be getting richer soon,
While some, just wishing to get salvation soon..

बुरा

ईसलिए की तुझे बुरा ना लग जाए,
जो थी वो शिकायते भी कभी नही की तुझ से।

If my feelings were a person

Only if my own feelings were a person,

I would've-

abandoned it in wild,
   for making me alone in the midst of mob..

Or, drugged it to senselessness,
   for making me numb..

Or, digged out the heart,
   and squeezed all the attachment from it..

Or, hammered the brain out,
   for all those toxic overthinking..

Or, poisoned it to death,
   for killing me all the seconds..

Or, strangled it to mortal,
   for taking my breathes away..

Or, freed it with forgiveness,
   being aware I'm not as cruel as him..

Love Again

If I have to fall in love again,
I will come to you..

despite being broken into pieces,
even if there's left a few..

I will come to you,
without knocking the door new..

अधूरा ही अच्छा

इश्क
  शायद
    अधूरा ही अच्छा होता है |

पा जो लो
  इश्क
    फिर इश्क कहां रहता है ||

My Expectations

Every time when I said *"Bye"*,
I was expecting *"Stay"* from you..
when I said *"I hate you"*,
I meant *"I love you"*..

I used to smile along you,
but in solitary, I used to cry..
after all the fights,
I came back for one more try..

In all our fights,
I was craving for love..
I tried all my best,
not to make it tough..

with all mine ignorance,
there was always care..

when I said *"don't talk"*,
I meant *"please hug"*..
but why in your heart of rock,
I tried looking for love, ugh!

Peace for Pieces

21

Seeking peace -
with all the broken pieces.

नहीं पता

नहीं पता क्या सही है -
तुमसे दूर जाना, या तुम्हें पा लेना ।

क्या दूर जाने से जीवन आसान हो जाएगा ?
क्या पाने से मुश्किलें नहीं आएंगी ??

नहीं समझ पाता क्या सही है -
तुमसे दूर जाना, या तुम्हें पा लेना ।।

Journey

What kind of journey I'm into?
Can't even go far from you,
Not even getting to you..

Pretending

Isn't life all about pretending?

Pretending to be living..
pretending to be happy..
pretending to be true..
pretending to be loyal..
pretending to be yourself..

the list continues.....

तमन्ना

बहुत कुछ गवा चुका हूँ मैं
बोहत कुछ पाने की तमन्ना में,

गम ही हाथ लगा मुझे
जीने की तमन्ना में,

अब बता दो कोई दवा, कब से बैठा हूं
इस गम को गवाने की तमन्ना में ||

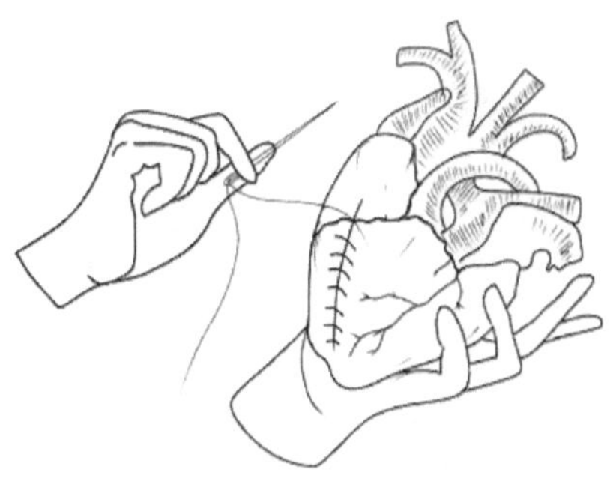

Blackout

If I cry my tears down,
in my feelings I get drown,
will you hold by hands and take me out,
Or leave me in midst of complete blackout?

तुम मानोगे नहीं

"तुम मानोगे नहीं पर सच है" कह के -
किसी और के लिए झूठ बोल जाती हो तुम ।

शायद भूल गए वो दिन -
जब यहीं झूठ मेरे लिए बोला करते थे तुम ॥

My Foul

Someday if you find me not on earth,
don't look for me among the stars..
seek me in depth of your heart,
I would have got rid of all the scars,
by leaving the body and my released soul.
count all our misdeeds as my foul..

Enemy

Whole world is my mate,
But my own heart is my enemy..

खुदा से बड़े

जितनी मिन्नतें और मन्नते की है मैंने तुम्हारे लिए,
इतना अगर खुदा को धरती पे बुलाने को करता,,
तो वो भी शायद कायनात अदा करते मुझे |

पर शायद तुम तो खुदा से भी बड़े निकले ||

Effort

It takes immense effort,
to make anything effortless..

Friends?

How can we be friends?

How can I talk about your new crush,
your new hangout place, and plans for the weekend..
despite knowing I won't top that list.
Yes, still it's the expectations of my beast..

Of your new partner - how can we do the bitching?
How can I, without feeling - scratch your itching..
despite knowing it will shatter my heart,
I don't know how to "fake the feelings" art..

we never were just friends,
and we can't be just friends,
but friendly..

Fictional Character

There's a fictional character inside me,
Who has won all the battles.

नक़ली

इन बड़े शहरो में
तो घास भी नक़ली बिकते हैं |

और तुम खाली जेब लेकर
सच्ची मोहब्बत ढूढने निकले थे ||

It matters

If I jump from the skyscraper,
my skull would burst & your memories would scatter,,
if I burn the soul and turn vapor,
your marks on me will fade and it matters..

If I get my wrist knifed,
my hands still have the feelings of your touches,,
if I take the cyanide,
my lips still get the feelings of your rushes..

If I suffocate myself,
nostrils don't want to forget your scent..
if I bury the bullet in chest oneself,
My heart has the copy of you my best..

I want to get away from this light,
while sleeping at night,,
while dreaming of you in my sight..

Innocence

When my innocence was betrayed,
I had trust on you and couldn't observe,,

when my heart was butchered,
I was repairing my nerves,,

when my dreams were crushed,
I was weaving them for our future,,

when I realized you are with other,
I couldn't accept I became a loser,,

when I got to know you have gone farther,
I was busy creating heaven for us..

आईना

मेरे कमरे की आईने में देख के
जब तुमने एक बार बाल सवारा था,
तब से उसमें तुम्हारी एक तस्वीर बन गई है।

आज भी जब मैं आईना देखता हूं,
तेरी सूरत साफ दिखती है मुझे ॥

Blade

I guess god also don't want to heal me!
seems he knows more than me about my sane..

seems he is afraid if he heals me,
I will go back to the blade again that gave me the pain..

Silence

After being shattered heart,
why do people turn silent?
with all those loud noise in chest,
why do lips get sealed without any accent?

I guess that's because they keep talking,
with their virtual version of the one,
who murdered their feelings without any gun,,
with the one who turned their eyes blind,
at Least they can argue with them in mind..

those silences are not actually silence,
they are actually a loud bang but with balance..

ग़रीब

इतने ग़रीब हुए हम,
कि अपनी मोहब्बत को नीलामियों से बचा ना सके |

काश दिल की दौलत से मोहब्बत चल पाती ||

Autumn

You return like autumn for a period of time
And I fall like leaves every time

मिलते-जुलते

कितने मिलते-जुलते हैं हम दोनों?

प्यार का नाम लेकर हम दोनों ने,
जिंदगी का एक बहुत बड़ा काम साथ मिल के किया हमने |

बड़े प्यार से बरबाद किया एक शख्स को,
उसने मुझको, और मैंने खुद को ||

बहुत मिलते-जुलते हैं हम दोनो !

Cloud in Lungs

Lit up one more cigarette,
oh I forgot it's 15th or 27th..
I may regret it later in life,
But I need this in right event.

My heart is looking into some unknown scene,
that's giving me the immense pain..
the mass of smoke that I inhale,
to put cloud in lungs so I can blind my heart..

Dripping

Why am I here? What are all these?
a pretty lady caressing my hand.
beeping sound with the rhythm of my heartbeats.
oh, I feel a pinch; she's putting a band.

am I supposed to be here?
was it again the moment of shocker?
otherwise, why would my eyes get teary?
oh yes, I got attacked by my heart's monster!

all these green curtains and the medical equipment
are asking me, "Why this treatment?"
But my ailment, dear doctor, isn't quite clear.
It's the failure of love, a malady I hold dear..

The heartbreak hit me, oh so severely,
like a hurricane in the midst of serenity..
now I'm trapped in this sterile domain,
trying to mend a heart that's broken in vain..

ख्वाहिश

* फ़वाहिश : बुरे काम

उसके सामने तो कुछ बोल ना सके,
पर कागज़ों पर लिखने की फ़वाहिश* है अब मुझे।

जीते जी तो जी ना सके,
मरने के बाद जिंदा रहने की ख्वाहिश है अब मुझे॥

* फ़वाहिश : बुरे काम

Sweet Hurt

** to measure*

Sweetheart, my heart have got some sweet hurt
It shouldn't but even in pain it feels pleasure

your hands are soaked with the bloods of my feelings
still my bloody soul seeks your touches and admeasure*

the eyes you use to stare at someone
my eyes In them searches for my figure

the lips you use for my curse and misery
my lips want them on themselves for century

** to measure*

बहुत दूर कितना दूर होता है?

सोचता हूं चला जाऊं दूर,
तुमसे बहुत दूर -
दूर इतना कि फिर तुम याद ना आओ |
पर ये बहुत दूर कितना दूर होता है?

रात की चादर में छुप कर भटकता,
ख्वाबों की दुनिया में खोता रहता |
क्या इंतजार ये कभी थमेगी ?
क्या तुम्हारी यादें कभी भी मिटेंगी ?

अपनी तलाश में खो जाऊं,
तुम्हारी यादों से बच पाऊं,,
पर दिल का ये सवाल सदा रहता है -
कि ये बहुत दूर कितना दूर होता है?

Cremate

When I die,
Please cremate me in books.

so I can get the scent I have been smelling,
so my soul can get painted in letters I have been reading,,

let the pages burn like the fire of my passion,
In the ashes, my spirit, forever in literary fashion,,

may the words that consumed me find their way,
to rise as stories anew, with the light of each day..

Sober

Even when I was sober, I was high on your love.
in the starry night, you were all I dreamt of.

Even when I was far from you, my heart was close to you.
in every thought, in every moment, my love for you grew.

In solitude and in the midst of life's grand show.
you were the constant, the one I'll always know..

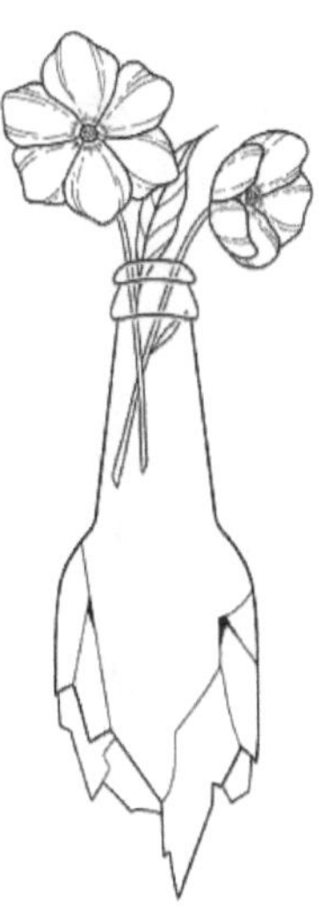

Cry the heart out

When you are hurt,
And eyes don't shed tears,,
When there's load in heart,
And you can't share it with peers,,
On the paper, cry the words out..

खौफ

खौफ मौत का नहीं है अब मुझे,
इतना प्यार जिंदगी से हुआ ही नहीं।

मेरे जाने के बाद जो जवाबदेही होगी,
उसका खौफ सताती है मुझे॥

Liabilities

These memories -
which we created as assets for future,
have turned into liabilities..

laughter and love, once a currency so rich,
now a debt, a reminder, an emotional stitch..

these memories, though heavy, need not define our fate,,
they can be stepping stones, a path to recreate..

बर्बाद

बड़ी आसानी से उनहोने
"बर्बाद" का ठप्पा हम पे लगा दिया |

और मेरी इश्क का जुनून तो देखो -
उनकी बात सच करने को
हमने खुद को बर्बाद करने का ठान लिया ||

Traffic Light

Why do people call it red light?

Although there are three,
one of them, the green,
remain lit long & bright,
and asks us to be free,
still we call it red light..

May be because we only focus on-
what stops us from from being free?

Coffee

If I die tomorrow, oh divinity
in next life I don't wish to live for infinity

I want to born again as a coffee
I expect it to be a short but sweet story

and put me in my beloved's hands
wait, I may hurt her if I spill

so instead of hot, make me cold
at least then I may touch her lips while my life ends..

Why She?

"Why do you think she's the one?"

Because -

every time I try to go far,
I end up going towards her..
Every night I sleep,
I wake-up dreaming about her..

after deciding not to see,
I wish to universe for her glance..
after deciding not to think,
I pray to god for one more chance..

रह गए

सुनहरे सारे ख्वाब मेरे
बुरे सपने बन के रह गए ।
जिसे कहते थे वो पराये
वो उनके अपने बन के रह गए ॥

फ़िर से एक बार दिल में मेरे
चढ़ा था शुरूर दीवानगी का ।
पर इस दीवानगी का भी किस्मत तो देखो
बस काग़ाज़ो के पन्ने बन के रह गए ॥

Home

Leaving the home that life gave,
with godly figures called parents
I started wandering in search,
whole heartedly with vibrance,
for a new home in someone's heart..

But when I got hurt from all the means,
got abandoned from my dream shelter,,
only with heart full of love
why did I expect without any treasure,
for a new home in someone's heart..

Instincts

When instincts roar, thoughts churn in a spin,
overthinking's grip, like a vice, draws me in,,

peace of mind departs, as I bid it adieu,,
in this whirlwind of thoughts, I'm lost without a clue..

मर्ज़

मर्ज़ क्या है पता नहीं |
शायद इसका कोई दवा नहीं ||

पर मर्ज़ इतनी बड़ी भी नहीं,
कि उनके एक बार पूछ लेने से -
ठीक ना हो ||

Dumb Love

This love thing must be dumb..
without anesthesia for making numb,,

people steal, without taking something from us..
people hurt, Without hitting on us..

without taking any steps, We reach somewhere..
and even going far, we reach nowhere..

starts with lies, and ends due to lies..
without shedding tears, heart cries..

try harder but you can't overcome..
yes mate, this love thing must be dumb..

Weakness

Trembling hands!
fumbling voice!
shivering body !
shattering heart!

are the proof that-
unknowingly you became my weakness..

अब क्या शिकवा

हार के दिल अपना जीतने की तमन्ना थी,
पर जीत के बदले हार मिली तो अब क्या शिकवा ।

तुम अपनी मर्जी से आ गए, अपनी मर्जी से आ गए,,
मेरी ना कभी सुनी तुमने, तो अब क्या शिकवा ॥

जिद्दी तुम भी थे, जिद्दी था मैं भी,,
किसी एक की जिद्द ना चली तो अब क्या शिकवा ॥।

मेरे पास

ये दर्द और ये यादें,
नहीं भूलना चाहता मैं |

इनके अलावा कुछ भी नहीं मेरे पास,
जो उसने दिया मुझे ||

Destiny

As the destiny of, a glass is to break,
attachments' destiny is heartbreak,,

unaware of this, I made a mistake,,
I kept loving, while you kept being fake..

Forgiveness

If I have to seek forgiveness,
what should I be sorry for?

For what I became?
or for what I couldn't??

For what I said?
or for what I couldn't??

सूरज चाँद

सूरज ने मुझे हँसते हुए देखा है, चाँद ने रोते देखा है,,
तेरी यादों की भीड़ में खोते देखा है।

भले ही कोई और हो आज वहाँ,
मेरे ख्वाबों में मैंने, खुद को तेरी बाहों में सोते देखा है ॥

Starve Myself

Uncontrollably when my anger develops,
blood gets poisonous throughout my veins,,

adrenaline starts rushing from top to toe,
then my eyes can't differentiate friend & foe,,

I starve myself to get low on energy,
with hope to match with others my synergy..

दिल मांस के

फट जाते गर बने जो होते दिल मांस के
पर कमबख्त या तो ये पत्थर के होते है, या कांच के
ऐसे ही नहीं एक दिल दूसरे दिल को तोड़ते है ||

We don't talk anymore

On bad days
my heart wants to talk to you,
and share it all with you.

but then I realize
we don't talk anymore,
and my heart shatters
making the day worse..

चांद-तारे

चांद-तारे तोड़ने की बात
तो सिर्फ कहानियाँ है |

खुद को तोड़ के प्यार किया तुमसे,
क्या इतना काफ़ी नहीं है ?

Heartless

When you give heart to someone,
they become heartless..

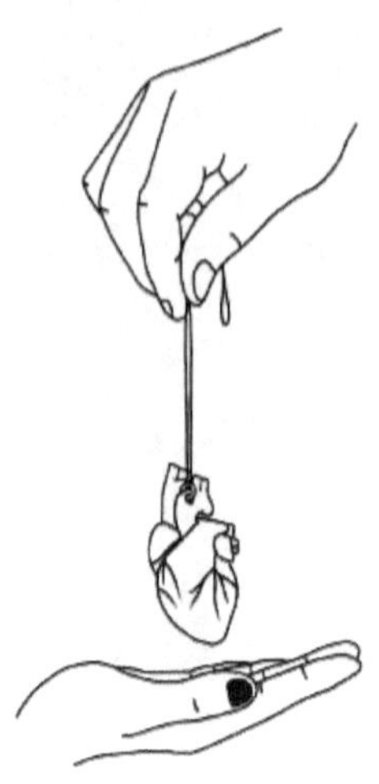

इज्जत

नहीं कहा उसने कि इश्क है तुमसे।
ना ही वो मुझे दूर होने दिया खुद से॥

ऐसा कर के मेरी इश्क की इज्जत रखी ?
या मुझको उसने दूर किया मुझसे ??

Blood on my hands

With the weapon of responsibilities,
when I killed all those dreams..
with the weapon of fear to be judged,
when I suppressed all those screams..

using the weapon of speaking truths,
when I strangled those relations..
by giving love to unlovables,
when I butchered all my emotions..

I got blood on my hands.

lies

I just wish

  not to find
    the truth

     about the lies
      they told me

साबित

कैसे कहु प्यार नहीं था उनको हमसे?
मेरे सारे शक सच साबित किये उन्होने !

Wish

77

I wish,
my wishes wouldn't just remain wishes..

चार

इस चार दिन की जिंदगी में
चार लम्हों का प्यार हुआ,
और चार जन्मो की जुदाई !

ऐ जिंदगी

क्यू रोज आखे नाम कर देते हो,
क्यू रोज भीड मी तन्हा कर देते हो |
क्यों खुद से मुझे अलग कर देते हो,
ऐ जिंदगी आज ना तुम बदलना ||

आजे वो आने वाले हैं, आने दो,
बातें करेंगे, करने दो |
लगे हाथ अपनी भी दिल की बात कर लेना,
ऐ जिंदगी आज कुछ ना तुम छुपाना ||

I'm fine

"How are you?" stands as one of the most frequently asked questions globally.

And "I'm fine" is probably the most faked answer.

It often carries a deeper truth — a response crafted to mask genuine emotions.

Imagine if we all just said how we really felt, and if the asker genuinely cared. Life might get a bit simpler with a touch of honesty and understanding.

तेरी याद

अजीब है तेरी याद भी,
पल भर में सब कुछ भुला देती है..

तेरे सिवा !!

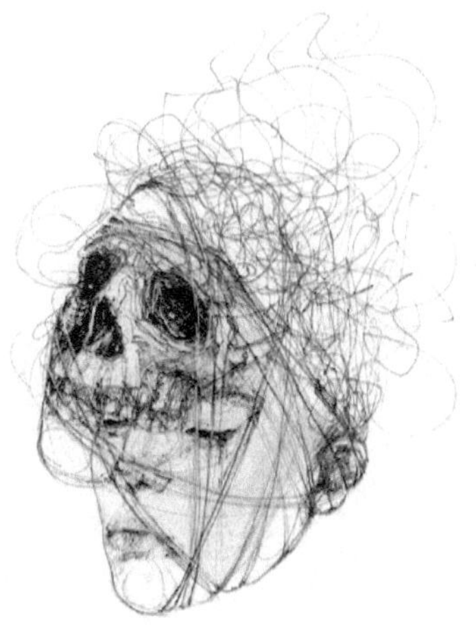

शिकायतें

शिकायतें तो बहुत हैं तुमसे,
क्योंकि प्यार भी तुमसे है।

प्यार ना होता,
तो शिकायतें भी नहीं होतीं।।

The Last Kiss

In midst of hilly dark night
love between us was at liss*
after that chaotic but calm Fight
alcohol was in it's vis **

Did you know how it tasted?
Yes, the taste of our last kiss,
it bore the taste of betrayal..
 a kiss of grief, once pure bliss..

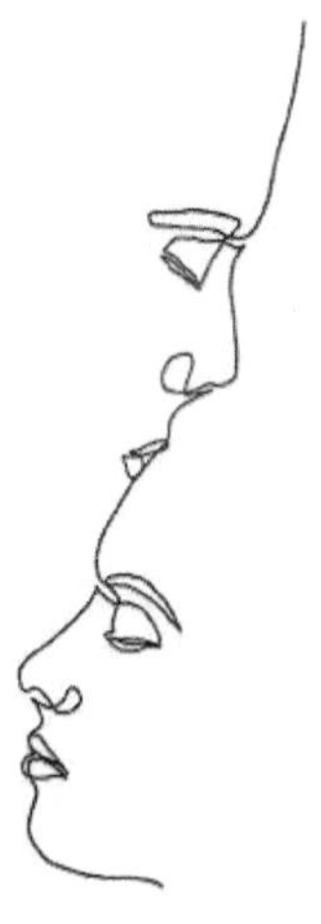

**liss: ease*
***vis: strength*

आना हो

थक गए हैं अब इंतजार करते करते,
जब आना हो तो आना ढेर सारी फुरसत लेकर।

ना भी आओ तो गम नहीं,
काट लेंगे जिंदगी तुम्हारा नाम लेकर ॥

All Good, Always Good!